THIS BOOK BELONGS TO

_____

START DATE

_____

SHE READS TRUTH

EXECUTIVE

FOUNDER/CHIEF EXECUTIVE OFFICER
Raechel Myers

CO-FOUNDER/CHIEF CONTENT OFFICER
Amanda Bible Williams

CHIEF OPERATING OFFICER
Ryan Myers

ASSISTANT TO THE EXECUTIVES
Taura Ryan

EDITORIAL

EDITORIAL DIRECTOR
Jessica Lamb

MANAGING EDITOR
Beth Joseph, MDiv

DIGITAL MANAGING EDITOR
Oghosa Iyamu, MDiv

ASSOCIATE EDITORS
Lindsey Jacobi, MDiv
Tameshia Williams, ThM

EDITORIAL ASSISTANT
Hannah Little, MTS

MARKETING

CUSTOMER JOURNEY
MARKETING MANAGER
Megan Gibbs

PRODUCT MARKETING MANAGER
Wesley Chandler

SOCIAL MEDIA STRATEGIST
Taylor Krupp

CREATIVE

CREATIVE DIRECTOR
Amy Dennis

ART DIRECTORS
Kelsea Allen
Aimee Lindamood

DESIGNERS
Abbey Benson
Amanda Brush, MA
Annie Glover
Lauren Haag

OPERATIONS

OFFICE MANAGER
Nicole Quirion

PROJECT ASSISTANT
Mary Beth Montgomery

SHIPPING

SHIPPING MANAGER
Elizabeth Thomas

FULFILLMENT LEAD
Cait Baggerman

FULFILLMENT SPECIALISTS
Kajsa Matheny
Ashley Richardson
Noe Sanchez

SUBSCRIPTION INQUIRIES
orders@shereadstruth.com

COMMUNITY SUPPORT

COMMUNITY SUPPORT MANAGER
Kara Hewett, MOL

COMMUNITY SUPPORT SPECIALISTS
Katy McKnight
Heather Vollono
Margot Williams

CONTRIBUTOR

SPECIAL THANKS
Lauren Gloyne

@SHEREADSTRUTH

Download the
She Reads Truth app,
available for iOS
and Android

Subscribe to the
She Reads Truth podcast

SHEREADSTRUTH.COM

This book was printed offset in Nashville, Tennessee, on 70# Lynx Opaque. Cover is 100# Cougar Cpaque with a soft touch lamination.

RUTH

SHE READS TRUTH

All are
welcome in
the kingdom
of God.

Raechel Myers
FOUNDER/CHIEF
EXECUTIVE OFFICER

A t 7:00 this morning I kissed my husband and kids goodbye, poured my first cup of coffee for the day, then crawled back into my bed to read the book of Ruth. I ended up reading it three times in that sitting (a full read-through only takes about fourteen minutes!). Each time, I noticed something different about Ruth, about Naomi, and about God.

At 10:00 this morning I joined our team in the She Reads Truth conference room. Our managing editor shared her heart for the content of this book and reading plan, and our book designer showed us how the book of Ruth moved her toward the color scheme and photos that set the stage for the reading experience you now hold in your hands. And do you know what else they pitched in this meeting? That you would read the book of Ruth three times in the coming two weeks. I couldn't help but smile at God's attention to detail—in my story, in Ruth's, and in yours, too.

At 3:00 this afternoon I sat down to write this letter to you. I'm still thinking about our meeting this morning and our conversations about the book of Ruth. It has met many of us on the team in such personal ways. The book of Ruth is so much more than a story about marriage or loyalty or family dynamics. Ruth's story is a demonstration of the gospel. It teaches us that all are welcome in the kingdom of God—that we are all wanted.

So, whatever time it is where you are as you read this letter today, I hope it encourages you to know that our team has prayed for you over and over as you begin this study. We hope this Study Book, and the Reader's Edition of Ruth we've included with it, will serve you well in your time in God's Word over the next two weeks. You'll find some helpful extras along the way (including a beautiful one called "God's Heart for the Vulnerable" on page 68), and we've made lots of space for you to take notes and reflect as you go. As you read about the life and legacy of Ruth, may you see the ways God brings meaning to family and loss, provision and work, hardships and community.

It's 4:00 now, and I'm signing this letter with a prayer for you. God, show her your gospel in your book of Ruth.

At She Reads Truth, we believe in pairing the inherently beautiful Word of God with the aesthetic beauty it deserves. Each of our resources is thoughtfully and artfully designed to highlight the beauty, goodness, and truth of Scripture in a way that reflects the themes of each curated reading plan.

For this Study Book, our team chose a color that represents the calmness and warmth of God's provision and care for Ruth and Naomi against the backdrop of Israel's sinful behavior and consequences in the book of Judges.

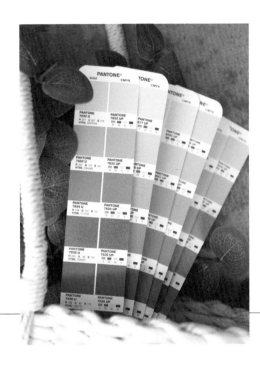

The book of Ruth is a story of how people both within the covenant community of Israel and outside of it were invited into God's kingdom. To represent this invitation we all have in God, we created a custom photo shoot focused on a welcoming gathering. Throughout the book, you'll see process photos of the gathering being set up. These photographs represent the journey of faith present in the middle of Ruth and Naomi's circumstances, as well as the place and abundance God provided.

HOW TO USE THIS BOOK

She Reads Truth is a community of women dedicated to reading the Word of God every day. In this **Ruth** reading plan, we will look at the book of Ruth to understand God's redemption, covenant faithfulness, and care for all who trust in Him.

READ & REFLECT

Your **Ruth** Study Book focuses primarily on Scripture, with bonus resources to facilitate deeper engagement with God's Word.

SCRIPTURE READING

Designed for a Monday start, this Study Book presents the book of Ruth in daily readings, along with additional passages curated to show how themes from the main reading can be found throughout Scripture.

❧ *Additional passages are marked in your daily reading with the Going Deeper heading.*

REFLECTION

Each weekday features space for personal notes and prayer, with an additional moment of reflection to conclude the plan.

COMMUNITY & CONVERSATION

You can start reading this book at any time! If you want to join women from Jackson to Japan as they read along with you, the She Reads Truth community will start Day 1 of **Ruth** on Monday, September 12, 2022.

 SHE READS TRUTH APP

Devotionals corresponding to each daily reading can be found in the **Ruth** reading plan on the She Reads Truth app. New devotionals will be published each weekday once the plan begins on Monday, September 12, 2022. You can use the app to participate in community discussion, download free lock screens for Weekly Truth memorization, and more.

GRACE DAY

Use Saturdays to catch up on your reading, pray, and rest in the presence of the Lord.

WEEKLY TRUTH

Sundays are set aside for Scripture memorization.

See tips for memorizing Scripture on page 92.

EXTRAS

This book features additional tools to help you gain a deeper understanding of the text.

Find a complete list of extras on page 10.

 SHEREADSTRUTH.COM

The **Ruth** reading plan and devotionals will also be available at SheReadsTruth.com as the community reads each day. Invite your family, friends, and neighbors to read along with you!

 SHE READS TRUTH PODCAST

Subscribe to the She Reads Truth podcast and join our founders and their guests each week as they talk about the beauty, goodness, and truth they find in Scripture.

 *Podcast episodes 145 and 146 for our **Ruth** series release on Mondays beginning September 12, 2022.*

TABLE OF CONTENTS

The book of Ruth was originally passed down through oral tradition and later read aloud in its entirety during Jewish festivals. Find the Ruth Reader's Edition insert in your Study Book. Take time before you begin Day 1 to read the narrative in its entirety. It only takes about fourteen minutes to read Ruth.

EXTRAS

WEEK 1

WEEK 2

KEY VERSE

THE WOMEN SAID TO NAOMI, "BLESSED BE
THE LORD, WHO HAS NOT LEFT YOU WITHOUT
A FAMILY REDEEMER TODAY. MAY HIS NAME
BECOME WELL KNOWN IN ISRAEL."

———

RUTH 4:14

SHE READS RUTH

**TIME TO
READ RUTH**
14 minutes

The book of Ruth is set "during the time of the judges" (Ru 1:1), a period of social and religious disorder when "everyone did whatever seemed right to him" (Jdg 17:6). Historically, this era bridged the time between the conquest of the land under Joshua's leadership and the rise of King David, whose genealogy forms the conclusion of the book. The book of Ruth opens with a famine in the land and ends with the birth of Obed, the grandfather of King David (likely between 1150 BC and 1100 BC).

A LITTLE BACKGROUND

The book of Ruth gets its name from one of its principal characters, a Moabite woman named Ruth, an ancestor of David and Jesus. After reading the book of Judges, which paints a dark and depressing picture of Israel, the story of Ruth comes as a welcome relief. Although the book is relatively short, it is rich in examples of kindness, faith, and patience. Ruth is one of the five scrolls that was to be read during the Jewish festivals, in particular the Festival of Weeks.

MESSAGE & PURPOSE

The book of Ruth demonstrates how the Lord shows His covenant faithfulness to His undeserving people, often in surprising ways. The genealogy of David at the end of the book shows that the Lord worked through this story to provide for His people's need for a king.

A correlation is sometimes made between the redemption of Ruth by Boaz and the redemption of sinners by Christ. Because of God's covenant faithfulness, He has provided, in Jesus, the Redeemer we all need.

GIVE THANKS FOR THE BOOK OF RUTH

Ruth's covenantal faithfulness to Naomi and to God showed that those who were not ethnic Israelites could be incorporated into the people of God through faith. If a Moabite widow who joined herself to the Lord could be accepted, there was hope for other Gentiles as well (Is 56:3–7). The book of Ruth effectively answered questions that some Israelites may have raised over the legitimacy of the Davidic line, given David's Moabite roots, and it also serves as a demonstration of Paul's later statement that there is "no distinction between Jew and Greek" when it comes to the gospel (Rm 10:12).

JOSHUA, JUDGES, RUTH

To understand the book of Ruth, it helps to remember its place in Israel's history. The book of Ruth comes directly after the books of Joshua and Judges in our Christian canon. Her story stands in contrast to the unfaithfulness of God's people during the time they were settling into the land God had given. When read together, the books of Joshua, Judges, and Ruth tell a story of great hope and the faithfulness of God toward His people.

JOSHUA

In the book of Joshua, the Israelites are repeatedly called to worship the Lord and serve Him only.

After God's people endured over four hundred years in Egypt, followed by forty years of wandering in the wilderness, the Lord raised up Joshua to lead Israel into the promised land.

Joshua led a successful conquest, Israel took the land of Canaan, and the twelve tribes began to settle there.

"Therefore, fear the Lord and worship him in sincerity and truth. Get rid of the gods your fathers worshiped beyond the Euphrates River and in Egypt, and worship the Lord. But if it doesn't please you to worship the Lord, choose for yourselves today: Which will you worship—the gods your ancestors worshiped beyond the Euphrates River or the gods of the Amorites in whose land you are living? As for me and my family, we will worship the Lord."

JOSHUA 24:14–15

JUDGES

Judges describes how Israel forsook the Lord and adopted the worship practices of the Canaanites.

Israel experienced chaotic and catastrophic consequences due to their rebellion. This period was marked by repeated cycles of unprecedented violence and oppression. Though God raised up judges as deliverers, they were unable to reverse this trend and some even became part of the problem.

Israel's downward spiral of rebellion led them to become almost unrecognizable as the people of God.

In those days there was no king in Israel; everyone did whatever seemed right to him.

JUDGES 21:25

RUTH

In the book of Ruth, a Moabite woman embraces the God of Israel.

During the time of the judges, famine sent Naomi's family away from Bethlehem to Moab, where one of her sons married a woman named Ruth.

When Naomi and Ruth were widowed, Ruth, a Moabite, pledged to stay with Naomi, an Israelite, and embrace the God of Israel.

As destitute, widowed refugees in one of the darkest periods of Israel's history, Ruth and Naomi were vulnerable and in need of redemption.

Ruth married an Israelite named Boaz and gave birth to Obed, King David's grandfather. From the line of Ruth and David would come Jesus, the Savior of the world.

Ruth, Naomi, and Boaz demonstrate God's covenant love and faithfulness.

But Ruth replied: "Don't plead with me to abandon you or to return and not follow you. For wherever you go, I will go, and wherever you live, I will live; your people will be my people, and your God will be my God."

RUTH 1:16

Naomi's Family in Moab

NAOMI'S FAMILY IN MOAB

¹ During the time of the judges, there was a famine in the land. A man left Bethlehem in Judah with his wife and two sons to stay in the territory of Moab for a while. ² The man's name was Elimelech, and his wife's name was Naomi. The names of his two sons were Mahlon and Chilion. They were Ephrathites from Bethlehem in Judah. They entered the fields of Moab and settled there. ³ Naomi's husband, Elimelech, died, and she was left with her two sons. ⁴ Her sons took Moabite women as their wives: one was named Orpah and the second was named Ruth. After they lived in Moab about ten years, ⁵ both Mahlon and Chilion also died, and the woman was left without her two children and without her husband.

📖 GOING DEEPER

JUDGES 2:11–19

¹¹ The Israelites did what was evil in the LORD's sight. They worshiped the Baals ¹² and abandoned the LORD, the God of their ancestors, who had brought them out of Egypt. They followed other gods from the surrounding peoples and bowed down to them. They angered the LORD, ¹³ for they abandoned him and worshiped Baal and the Ashtoreths.

¹⁴ The LORD's anger burned against Israel, and he handed them over to marauders who raided them. He sold them to the enemies around them, and they could no longer resist their enemies. ¹⁵ Whenever the Israelites went out, the LORD was against them and brought disaster on them, just as he had promised and sworn to them. So they suffered greatly.

¹⁶ The LORD raised up judges, who saved them from the power of their marauders, ¹⁷ but they did not listen to their judges. Instead, they prostituted themselves with other gods, bowing down to them. They quickly turned from the way of their ancestors, who had walked in obedience to the LORD's commands. They did not do as their ancestors did.

¹⁸ Whenever the LORD raised up a judge for the Israelites, the LORD was with him and saved the people from the power of their enemies while the judge was still alive. The LORD was moved to pity whenever they groaned because of those who were oppressing and afflicting them. ¹⁹ Whenever the judge died, the Israelites would act even more corruptly than their ancestors, following other gods to serve them and bow in worship to them. They did not turn from their evil practices or their obstinate ways.

JUDGES 21:25

In those days there was no king in Israel; everyone did whatever seemed right to him.

1 TIMOTHY 5:4–8

⁴ But if any widow has children or grandchildren, let them learn to practice godliness toward their own family first and to repay their parents, for this pleases God.

⁵ The widow who is truly in need and left all alone has put her hope in God

and continues night and day in her petitions and prayers; ⁶ however, she who is self-indulgent is dead even while she lives. ⁷ Command this also, so that they will be above reproach. ⁸ But if anyone does not provide for his own family, especially for his own household, he has denied the faith and is worse than an unbeliever.

Notes

7-11-24

Poor Naomi experienced such heartache losing her husband & her two sons.

My past is like the Israelites, worshipping other gods & putting other things in front of God. But God, thank you for pulling me out of that pit, for forgiveness & grace.

It's hard to imagine the Israelites turning from God after all God had done for them, but that's much like our lives. We choose to leave the peace & comfort of Christ (the peace & comfort that is even given during difficult times) for worldly pleasures that don't last & that will fail us. God will NEVER fail us - His promises remain & we can rest in the hope & certainty of eternity! Hallelujah!

Ruth's Loyalty to Naomi

RUTH 1:6–18

RUTH'S LOYALTY TO NAOMI

⁶ She and her daughters-in-law set out to return from the territory of Moab, because she had heard in Moab that the LORD had paid attention to his people's need by providing them food. ⁷ She left the place where she had been living, accompanied by her two daughters-in-law, and traveled along the road leading back to the land of Judah.

⁸ Naomi said to them, "Each of you go back to your mother's home.

May the LORD show kindness to you

as you have shown to the dead and to me. ⁹ May the LORD grant each of you rest in the house of a new husband." She kissed them, and they wept loudly.

¹⁰ They said to her, "We insist on returning with you to your people."

¹¹ But Naomi replied, "Return home, my daughters. Why do you want to go with me? Am I able to have any more sons who could become your husbands? ¹² Return home, my daughters. Go on, for I am too old to have another husband. Even if I thought there was still hope for me to have a husband tonight and to

bear sons, ¹³ would you be willing to wait for them to grow up? Would you restrain yourselves from remarrying? No, my daughters, my life is much too bitter for you to share, because the LORD's hand has turned against me." ¹⁴ Again they wept loudly, and Orpah kissed her mother-in-law, but Ruth clung to her. ¹⁵ Naomi said, "Look, your sister-in-law has gone back to her people and to her gods. Follow your sister-in-law."

¹⁶ But Ruth replied:

> Don't plead with me to abandon you
> or to return and not follow you.
> For wherever you go, I will go,
> and wherever you live, I will live;
> your people will be my people,
> and your God will be my God.
> ¹⁷ Where you die, I will die,
> and there I will be buried.
> May the LORD punish me,
> and do so severely,
> if anything but death separates you and me.

¹⁸ When Naomi saw that Ruth was determined to go with her, she stopped talking to her.

♥ GOING DEEPER

PSALM 136:1–4

GOD'S LOVE IS ETERNAL

¹ Give thanks to the LORD, for he is good.
His faithful love endures forever.
² Give thanks to the God of gods.
His faithful love endures forever.
³ Give thanks to the Lord of lords.
His faithful love endures forever.
⁴ He alone does great wonders.
His faithful love endures forever.

PSALM 146:5–10

⁵ Happy is the one whose help is the God of Jacob,
whose hope is in the LORD his God,
⁶ the Maker of heaven and earth,
the sea and everything in them.
He remains faithful forever,
⁷ executing justice for the exploited
and giving food to the hungry.
The LORD frees prisoners.
⁸ The LORD opens the eyes of the blind.
The LORD raises up those who are oppressed.
The LORD loves the righteous.
⁹ The LORD protects resident aliens
and helps the fatherless and the widow,
but he frustrates the ways of the wicked.

¹⁰ The LORD reigns forever;
Zion, your God reigns for all generations.
Hallelujah!

EPHESIANS 2:11–13

UNITY IN CHRIST

¹¹ So, then, remember that at one time you were Gentiles in the flesh—called "the uncircumcised" by those called "the circumcised," which is done in the flesh by human hands. ¹² At that time you were without Christ, excluded from the citizenship of Israel, and foreigners to the covenants of promise, without hope and without God in the world. ¹³ But now in Christ Jesus, you who were far away have been brought near by the blood of Christ.

Notes

No matter who you are, where you come from, what you've done — you are ACCEPTED in the kingdom of Christ. You have a seat at the table, at <u>His</u> table. The best part is — I didn't earn that seat, & there is not a thing I could do to earn it. He wants me to be a family member at <u>His</u> table.

Oh how I want to have the determination & willingness of Ruth. Her dedication to her mother-in-law. I think about it in two scenarios- one being our willingness to cling to God & go & do whatever He would have us do. The other serving others - our family - grandparents, parents, siblings, one another in marriage, children & even strangers. Sometimes, often, I only want to do what is beneficial to me or convenient for me. I don't want to do that anymore. I want to be a servant for Jesus Christ.

Even in the midst of heartache & grieving, Ruth didn't hide in a corner or give up. She chose to stay with Naomi & never leave her. Like Jesus never leaves us - even when we're in pain, grieving, angry, confused & upset. He will never leave us.

NAMES IN RUTH

The book of Ruth is a compelling true story in redemption history. It's also beautiful literature that displays the art of deep, compact storytelling. Most of the characters have Hebrew names that seem to reflect their journey or part in the story. Turn back to this extra to reference the meanings of each name as you read the book of Ruth.

BOAZ
RU 2:1

In him there is might, or strength

CHILION
RU 1:2

Wasting away, sickly, or annihilation

ELIMELECH
RU 1:2

My God is king

MAHLON
RU 1:2

Weakness, sickly, or invalid

MARA
RU 1:20

Bitter

NAOMI
RU 1:2

Pleasant, kind

OBED
RU 4:17

Serving, worshiper

ORPAH
RU 1:4

Neck, rain cloud

RUTH
RU 1:4

Neighbor, friend, or companion

Naomi and Ruth Return

RUTH 1:19–22

[19] The two of them traveled until they came to Bethlehem. When they entered Bethlehem, the whole town was excited about their arrival and the local women exclaimed, "Can this be Naomi?"

[20] "Don't call me Naomi. Call me Mara," she answered, "for the Almighty has made me very bitter. [21] I went away full, but the LORD has brought me back empty. Why do you call me Naomi, since the LORD has opposed me, and the Almighty has afflicted me?"

[22] So Naomi came back from the territory of Moab with her daughter-in-law Ruth the Moabitess. They arrived in Bethlehem at the beginning of the barley harvest.

RUTH 2:1–3

RUTH AND BOAZ MEET

[1] Now Naomi had a relative on her husband's side. He was a prominent man of noble character from Elimelech's family. His name was Boaz.

[2] Ruth the Moabitess asked Naomi, "Will you let me go into the fields and gather fallen grain behind someone with whom I find favor?"

Naomi answered her, "Go ahead, my daughter." ³ So Ruth left and entered the field to gather grain behind the harvesters. She happened to be in the portion of the field belonging to Boaz, who was from Elimelech's family.

🔖 GOING DEEPER

ISAIAH 38:9–20

⁹ A poem by King Hezekiah of Judah after he had been sick and had recovered from his illness:

> ¹⁰ I said: In the prime of my life
> I must go to the gates of Sheol;
> I am deprived of the rest of my years.
> ¹¹ I said: I will never see the LORD,
> the LORD in the land of the living;
> I will not look on humanity any longer
> with the inhabitants of what is passing away.
> ¹² My dwelling is plucked up and removed from me
> like a shepherd's tent.
> I have rolled up my life like a weaver;
> he cuts me off from the loom.
> By nightfall you make an end of me.
> ¹³ I thought until the morning:
> He will break all my bones like a lion.
> By nightfall you make an end of me.
> ¹⁴ I chirp like a swallow or a crane;
> I moan like a dove.
> My eyes grow weak looking upward.
> Lord, I am oppressed; support me.

> ¹⁵ What can I say?
> He has spoken to me,
> and he himself has done it.
> I walk along slowly all my years
> because of the bitterness of my soul.
> ¹⁶ Lord, by such things people live,
> and in every one of them my spirit finds life;
> you have restored me to health
> and let me live.

It's no coincidence that Ruth was in Boaz's field to gather fallen grain. God places us in the exact places we need to be.

We need to be ready to accept or do what God has for us in those moments — to be ready, we should be seeking Christ & His will, studying His Word, seeking to be well-watered, even in times of drought.

God gives us the choice. The King of the universe allows us to freely choose to worship Him.

Hezekiah was ill & asked God for a sign that he would be healed.

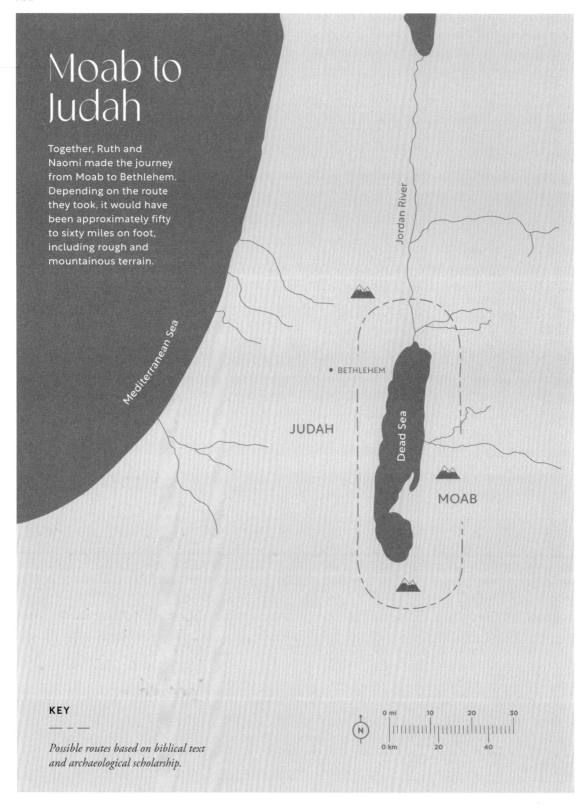

Moab to Judah

Together, Ruth and Naomi made the journey from Moab to Bethlehem. Depending on the route they took, it would have been approximately fifty to sixty miles on foot, including rough and mountainous terrain.

Mediterranean Sea

Jordan River

• BETHLEHEM

JUDAH

Dead Sea

MOAB

KEY

– – – –

Possible routes based on biblical text and archaeological scholarship.

N

0 mi   10   20   30

0 km   20   40

[17] Indeed, it was for my own well-being
that I had such intense bitterness;
but your love has delivered me
from the Pit of destruction,
for you have thrown all my sins behind your back.
[18] For Sheol cannot thank you;
Death cannot praise you.
Those who go down to the Pit
cannot hope for your faithfulness.
[19] The living, only the living can thank you,
as I do today;
a father will make your faithfulness known to children.

[20] The LORD is ready to save me;

we will play stringed instruments
all the days of our lives
at the house of the LORD.

PHILIPPIANS 3:8–11

[8] More than that, I also consider everything to be a loss in view of the surpassing value of knowing Christ Jesus my Lord. Because of him I have suffered the loss of all things and consider them as dung, so that I may gain Christ [9] and be found in him, not having a righteousness of my own from the law, but one that is through faith in Christ—the righteousness from God based on faith. [10] My goal is to know him and the power of his resurrection and the fellowship of his sufferings, being conformed to his death, [11] assuming that I will somehow reach the resurrection from among the dead.

WEEK 01

DAY

01
02
03
04 –
05
06
07

Boaz's Kindness to Ruth

[4] Later, when Boaz arrived from Bethlehem, he said to the harvesters, "The LORD be with you."

"The LORD bless you," they replied.

[5] Boaz asked his servant who was in charge of the harvesters, "Whose young woman is this?"

[6] The servant answered, "She is the young Moabite woman who returned with Naomi from the territory of Moab. [7] She asked, 'Will you let me gather fallen grain among the bundles behind the harvesters?' She came and has been on her feet since early morning, except that she rested a little in the shelter."

[8] Then Boaz said to Ruth, "Listen, my daughter. Don't go and gather grain in another field, and don't leave this one, but stay here close to my female servants. [9] See which field they are harvesting, and follow them. Haven't I ordered the young men not to touch you? When you are thirsty, go and drink from the jars the young men have filled."

[10] She fell facedown, bowed to the ground, and said to him, "Why have I found favor with you, so that you notice me, although I am a foreigner?"

[11] Boaz answered her, "Everything you have done for your mother-in-law since your husband's death has been fully reported to me: how you left your father and mother and your native land, and how you came to a people you didn't previously know. [12] May the LORD reward you for what you have done, and may you receive a full reward from the LORD God of Israel, under whose wings you have come for refuge."

[13] "My lord," she said, "I have found favor with you, for you have comforted and encouraged your servant, although I am not like one of your female servants."

[14] At mealtime Boaz told her, "Come over here and have some bread and dip it in the vinegar sauce." So she sat beside the harvesters, and he offered her roasted grain. She ate and was satisfied and had some left over.

[15] When she got up to gather grain, Boaz ordered his young men, "Let her even gather grain among the bundles, and don't humiliate her. [16] Pull out some stalks from the bundles for her and leave them for her to gather. Don't rebuke her." [17] So Ruth gathered grain in the field until evening. She beat out what she had gathered, and it was about twenty-six quarts of barley.

LEVITICUS 19:9–10

⁹ "When you reap the harvest of your land, you are not to reap to the very edge of your field or gather the gleanings of your harvest. ¹⁰ Do not strip your vineyard bare or gather its fallen grapes. Leave them for the poor and the resident alien; I am the Lᴏʀᴅ your God."

PSALM 36:7–9

⁷ How priceless your faithful love is, God!

People take refuge in the shadow of
    your wings.
⁸ They are filled from the abundance
    of your house.
You let them drink from your
    refreshing stream.

⁹ For the wellspring of life is with you.
By means of your light we see light.

MATTHEW 25:35–46

³⁵ "'For I was hungry and you gave me something to eat; I was thirsty and you gave me something to drink; I was a stranger and you took me in; ³⁶ I was naked and you clothed me; I was sick and you took care of me; I was in prison and you visited me.'

³⁷ "Then the righteous will answer him, 'Lord, when did we see you hungry and feed you, or thirsty and give you something to drink? ³⁸ When did we see you a stranger and take you in, or without clothes and clothe you? ³⁹ When did we see you sick, or in prison, and visit you?'

⁴⁰ "And the King will answer them, 'Truly I tell you, whatever you did for one of the least of these brothers and sisters of mine, you did for me.'

Help without others having to feel embarrassed. Just leave it for them to get.

glean - gather leftover harvest

It matters to God how we treat other believers in Christ.

[41] "Then he will also say to those on the left, 'Depart from me, you who are cursed, into the eternal fire prepared for the devil and his angels! [42] For I was hungry and you gave me nothing to eat; I was thirsty and you gave me nothing to drink; [43] I was a stranger and you didn't take me in; I was naked and you didn't clothe me, sick and in prison and you didn't take care of me.'

[44] "Then they too will answer, 'Lord, when did we see you hungry, or thirsty, or a stranger, or without clothes, or sick, or in prison, and not help you?'

[45] "Then he will answer them, 'Truly I tell you, whatever you did not do for one of the least of these, you did not do for me.'

[46] "And they will go away into eternal punishment, but the righteous into eternal life."

Notes

May the LORD show kindness to you as you have shown to the dead and to me.

Naomi and Ruth's Family Redeemer

RUTH 2:18–23

18 She picked up the grain and went into the town, where her mother-in-law saw what she had gleaned. She brought out what she had left over from her meal and gave it to her.

19 Her mother-in-law said to her, "Where did you gather barley today, and where did you work? May the LORD bless the man who noticed you."

Ruth told her mother-in-law whom she had worked with and said, "The name of the man I worked with today is Boaz."

20 Then Naomi said to her daughter-in-law, "May the LORD bless him because he has not abandoned his kindness to the living or the dead." Naomi continued, "The man is a close relative. He is one of our family redeemers."

21 Ruth the Moabitess said, "He also told me, 'Stay with my young men until they have finished all of my harvest.'"

22 So Naomi said to her daughter-in-law Ruth, "My daughter, it is good for you to work with his female servants, so that nothing will happen to you in another field." 23 Ruth stayed close to Boaz's female servants and gathered grain until the barley and the wheat harvests were finished. And she lived with her mother-in-law.

DEUTERONOMY 25:5–10

PRESERVING THE FAMILY LINE

⁵ When brothers live on the same property and one of them dies without a son, the wife of the dead man may not marry a stranger outside the family. Her brother-in-law is to take her as his wife, have sexual relations with her, and perform the duty of a brother-in-law for her. ⁶ The first son she bears will carry on the name of the dead brother, so his name will not be blotted out from Israel. ⁷ But if the man doesn't want to marry his sister-in-law, she is to go to the elders at the city gate and say, "My brother-in-law refuses to preserve his brother's name in Israel. He isn't willing to perform the duty of a brother-in-law for me." ⁸ The elders of his city will summon him and speak with him. If he persists and says, "I don't want to marry her," ⁹ then his sister-in-law will go up to him in the sight of the elders, remove his sandal from his foot, and spit in his face. Then she will declare, "This is what is done to a man who will not build up his brother's house." ¹⁰ And his family name in Israel will be "The house of the man whose sandal was removed."

PSALM 41:1–3

VICTORY IN SPITE OF BETRAYAL

For the choir director. A psalm of David.

¹ Happy is one who is considerate of the poor;
the LORD will save him in a day of adversity.
² The LORD will keep him and preserve him;
he will be blessed in the land.
You will not give him over to the desire of his enemies.
³ The LORD will sustain him on his sickbed;
you will heal him on the bed where he lies.

GALATIANS 6:9–10

⁹ Let us not get tired of doing good, for we will reap at the proper time if we don't give up. ¹⁰ Therefore, as we have opportunity, let us work for the good of all, especially for those who belong to the household of faith.

Notes

Grace

Take this day to catch
up on your reading, pray,
and rest in the presence
of the Lord.

Day

How priceless your
faithful love is, God!
People take refuge in the
shadow of your wings.

————

PSALM 36:7

Weekly Truth

SCRIPTURE IS GOD-BREATHED AND TRUE. WHEN WE MEMORIZE IT, WE CARRY HIS WORD WITH US WHEREVER WE GO.

This week we will work to memorize Ruth 4:14, our key verse for the book of Ruth. This verse reminds us of the message of Ruth and the hope of the gospel—we have not been left without a Redeemer.

THE WOMEN SAID TO NAOMI, "BLESSED BE
THE LORD, WHO HAS NOT LEFT YOU WITHOUT
A FAMILY REDEEMER TODAY. MAY HIS NAME
BECOME WELL KNOWN IN ISRAEL."

RUTH 4:14

See tips for memorizing Scripture on page 92.

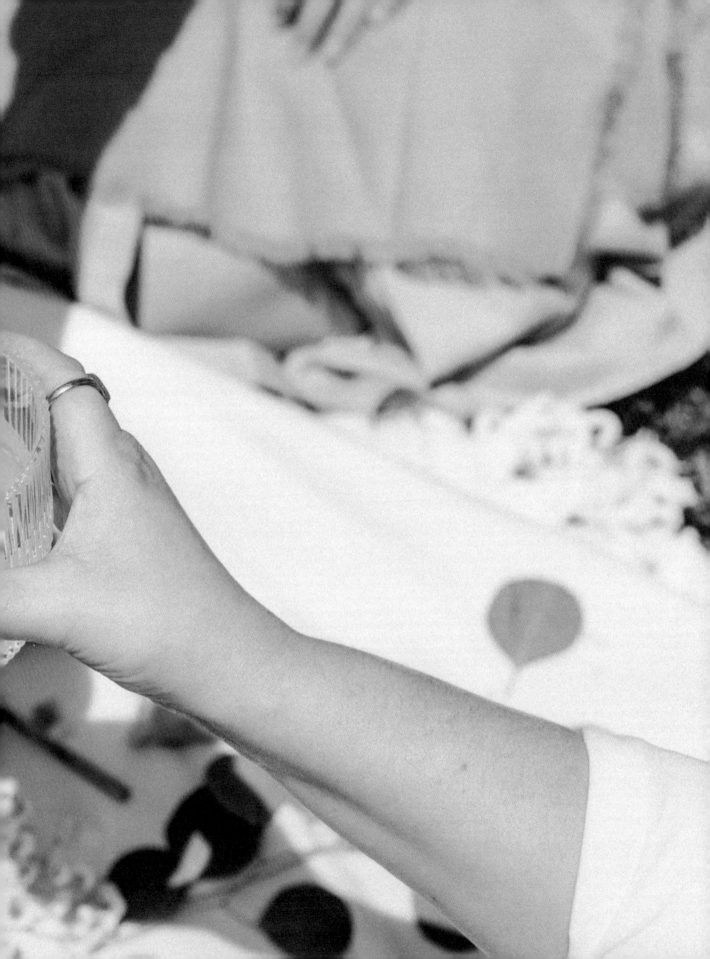

Ruth's Appeal to Boaz

RUTH 3:1–13

RUTH'S APPEAL TO BOAZ

[1] Ruth's mother-in-law Naomi said to her, "My daughter, shouldn't I find rest for you, so that you will be taken care of? [2] Now isn't Boaz our relative? Haven't you been working with his female servants? This evening he will be winnowing barley on the threshing floor. [3] Wash, put on perfumed oil, and wear your best clothes. Go down to the threshing floor, but don't let the man know you are there until he has finished eating and drinking. [4] When he lies down, notice the place where he's lying, go in and uncover his feet, and lie down. Then he will explain to you what you should do."

[5] So Ruth said to her, "I will do everything you say." [6] She went down to the threshing floor and did everything her mother-in-law had charged her to do. [7] After Boaz ate, drank, and was in good spirits, he went to lie down at the end of the pile of barley, and she came secretly, uncovered his feet, and lay down.

[8] At midnight, Boaz was startled, turned over, and there lying at his feet was a woman! [9] So he asked, "Who are you?"

"I am Ruth, your servant," she replied. "Take me under your wing, for you are a family redeemer."

¹⁰ Then he said, "May the LORD bless you, my daughter. You have shown more kindness now than before, because you have not pursued younger men, whether rich or poor. ¹¹ Now don't be afraid, my daughter.

I will do for you whatever you say, since all the people in my town know that you are a woman of noble character.

¹² Yes, it is true that I am a family redeemer, but there is a redeemer closer than I am. ¹³ Stay here tonight, and in the morning, if he wants to redeem you, that's good. Let him redeem you. But if he doesn't want to redeem you, as the LORD lives, I will. Now lie down until morning."

◗ GOING DEEPER

PROVERBS 31:10–31

IN PRAISE OF A WIFE OF NOBLE CHARACTER

¹⁰ Who can find a wife of noble character?
She is far more precious than jewels.
¹¹ The heart of her husband trusts in her,
and he will not lack anything good.
¹² She rewards him with good, not evil,
all the days of her life.
¹³ She selects wool and flax
and works with willing hands.
¹⁴ She is like the merchant ships,
bringing her food from far away.
¹⁵ She rises while it is still night
and provides food for her household
and portions for her female servants.
¹⁶ She evaluates a field and buys it;
she plants a vineyard with her earnings.
¹⁷ She draws on her strength
and reveals that her arms are strong.
¹⁸ She sees that her profits are good,
and her lamp never goes out at night.
¹⁹ She extends her hands to the spinning staff,
and her hands hold the spindle.
²⁰ Her hands reach out to the poor,
and she extends her hands to the needy.

NOTES

²¹ She is not afraid for her household when it snows,
for all in her household are doubly clothed.
²² She makes her own bed coverings;
her clothing is fine linen and purple.
²³ Her husband is known at the city gates,
where he sits among the elders of the land.
²⁴ She makes and sells linen garments;
she delivers belts to the merchants.
²⁵ Strength and honor are her clothing,
and she can laugh at the time to come.
²⁶ Her mouth speaks wisdom,
and loving instruction is on her tongue.
²⁷ She watches over the activities of her household
and is never idle.
²⁸ Her children rise up and call her blessed;
her husband also praises her:
²⁹ "Many women have done noble deeds,
but you surpass them all!"
³⁰ Charm is deceptive and beauty is fleeting,
but a woman who fears the LORD will be praised.
³¹ Give her the reward of her labor,
and let her works praise her at the city gates.

EPHESIANS 1:7–12

⁷ In him we have redemption through his blood, the forgiveness of our trespasses, according to the riches of his grace ⁸ that he richly poured out on us with all wisdom and understanding. ⁹ He made known to us the mystery of his will, according to his good pleasure that he purposed in Christ ¹⁰ as a plan for the right time—to bring everything together in Christ, both things in heaven and things on earth in him.

¹¹ In him we have also received an inheritance, because we were predestined according to the plan of the one who works out everything in agreement with the purpose of his will, ¹² so that we who had already put our hope in Christ might bring praise to his glory.

Notes

GLOSSARY
OF TERMS

BARLEY HARVEST

A grain harvest beginning as early as March or April and ripening around the time of Passover.

BETHLEHEM

A city in Israel, near Jerusalem, east of the Mediterranean Sea, where King David and Jesus were born. In Hebrew *beth lehem* means "house of bread."

FAMILY REDEEMER

Also known as a kinsman redeemer, one who is able to accept property and carry out legal affairs on behalf of a vulnerable relative. The act of "redeeming" (or redemption) occurs throughout Scripture as a saving activity.

GLEANING

The custom of allowing the poor to follow the harvesters in the field to gather fallen grain for themselves.

MOAB

The historical name for the mountainous region east of the Dead Sea. The Moabites worshiped many false gods. After the exodus, the Israelites passed through the land of Moab, where they were denied bread and water.

THRESHING FLOOR

A flat area used for separating the grain from the chaff during harvest.

WHEAT HARVEST

A grain harvest beginning as early as April or May and ripening around the time of Pentecost.

Ruth Waits for Redemption

RUTH 3:14–18

[14] So she lay down at his feet until morning but got up while it was still dark. Then Boaz said, "Don't let it be known that a woman came to the threshing floor." [15] And he told Ruth, "Bring the shawl you're wearing and hold it out." When she held it out, he shoveled six measures of barley into her shawl, and she went into the town.

[16] She went to her mother-in-law, Naomi, who asked her, "What happened, my daughter?"

Then Ruth told her everything the man had done for her. [17] She said, "He gave me these six measures of barley, because he said, 'Don't go back to your mother-in-law empty-handed.'"

[18] Naomi said, "My daughter, wait until you find out how things go, for he won't rest unless he resolves this today."

PSALM 37:3–7, 16–29

[3] Trust in the LORD and do what is good;
dwell in the land and live securely.
[4] Take delight in the LORD,
and he will give you your heart's desires.

[5] Commit your way to the LORD;
trust in him, and he will act,
[6] making your righteousness shine like the dawn,
your justice like the noonday.

[7] Be silent before the LORD and wait expectantly for him;
do not be agitated by one who prospers in his way,
by the person who carries out evil plans.

…

[16] The little that the righteous person has is better
than the abundance of many wicked people.
[17] For the arms of the wicked will be broken,
but the LORD supports the righteous.

[18] The LORD watches over the blameless all their days,
and their inheritance will last forever.
[19] They will not be disgraced in times of adversity;
they will be satisfied in days of hunger.

[20] But the wicked will perish;
the LORD's enemies, like the glory of the pastures,
will fade away—
they will fade away like smoke.

[21] The wicked person borrows and does not repay,
but the righteous one is gracious and giving.
[22] Those who are blessed by the LORD will inherit the land,
but those cursed by him will be destroyed.

[23] A person's steps are established by the LORD,
and he takes pleasure in his way.
[24] Though he falls, he will not be overwhelmed,
because the LORD supports him with his hand.

[25] I have been young and now I am old,
yet I have not seen the righteous abandoned
or his children begging for bread.
[26] He is always generous, always lending,
and his children are a blessing.

[27] Turn away from evil, do what is good,
and settle permanently.
[28] For the LORD loves justice
and will not abandon his faithful ones.
They are kept safe forever,
but the children of the wicked will be destroyed.
[29] The righteous will inherit the land
and dwell in it permanently.

PHILIPPIANS 4:4–9

[4] Rejoice in the Lord always. I will say it again: Rejoice! [5] Let your graciousness be known to everyone. The Lord is near. [6] Don't worry about anything, but in everything, through prayer and petition with thanksgiving, present your requests to God.

[7] And the peace of God, which surpasses all understanding, will guard your hearts and minds in Christ Jesus.

[8] Finally brothers and sisters, whatever is true, whatever is honorable, whatever is just, whatever is pure, whatever is lovely, whatever is commendable—if there is any moral excellence and if there is anything praiseworthy—dwell on these things. [9] Do what you have learned and received and heard from me, and seen in me, and the God of peace will be with you.

Notes

Boaz Redeems Ruth

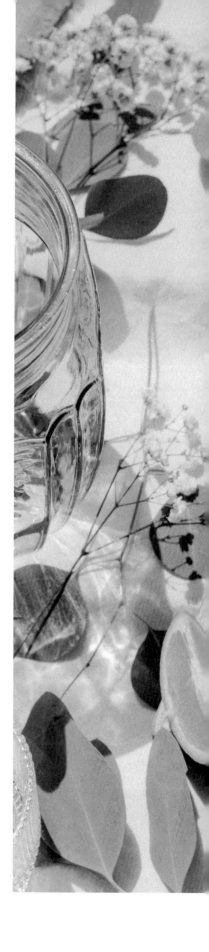

¹ Boaz went to the gate of the town and sat down there. Soon the family redeemer Boaz had spoken about came by. Boaz said, "Come over here and sit down." So he went over and sat down. ² Then Boaz took ten men of the town's elders and said, "Sit here." And they sat down. ³ He said to the redeemer, "Naomi, who has returned from the territory of Moab, is selling the portion of the field that belonged to our brother Elimelech. ⁴ I thought I should inform you: Buy it back in the presence of those seated here and in the presence of the elders of my people. If you want to redeem it, do it. But if you do not want to redeem it, tell me so that I will know, because there isn't anyone other than you to redeem it, and I am next after you."

"I want to redeem it," he answered.

⁵ Then Boaz said, "On the day you buy the field from Naomi, you will acquire Ruth the Moabitess, the wife of the deceased man, to perpetuate the man's name on his property."

⁶ The redeemer replied, "I can't redeem it myself, or I will ruin my own inheritance. Take my right of redemption, because I can't redeem it."

⁷ At an earlier period in Israel, a man removed his sandal and gave it to the other party in order to make any matter legally binding concerning the right of redemption or the exchange of property. This was the method of legally binding a transaction in Israel.

⁸ So the redeemer removed his sandal and said to Boaz, "Buy back the property yourself."

⁹ Boaz said to the elders and all the people, "You are witnesses today that I am buying from Naomi everything that belonged to Elimelech, Chilion, and Mahlon. ¹⁰ I have also acquired Ruth the Moabitess, Mahlon's widow, as my wife, to perpetuate the deceased man's name on his property, so that his name will not disappear among his relatives or from the gate of his hometown. You are witnesses today."

¹¹ All the people who were at the city gate, including the elders, said, "We are witnesses. May the LORD make the woman who is entering your house like Rachel and Leah, who together built the house of Israel. May you be powerful in Ephrathah and your name well known in Bethlehem. ¹² May your house become like the house of Perez, the son Tamar bore to Judah, because of the offspring the LORD will give you by this young woman."

◤ GOING DEEPER

PSALM 127

THE BLESSING OF THE LORD

A song of ascents. Of Solomon.

¹ Unless the LORD builds a house,
its builders labor over it in vain;
unless the LORD watches over a city,
the watchman stays alert in vain.
² In vain you get up early and stay up late,
working hard to have enough food—
yes, he gives sleep to the one he loves.

³ Sons are indeed a heritage from the LORD,
offspring, a reward.
⁴ Like arrows in the hand of a warrior
are the sons born in one's youth.
⁵ Happy is the man who has filled his quiver with them.
They will never be put to shame
when they speak with their enemies at the city gate.

1 PETER 1:18–19

¹⁸ For you know that you were redeemed from your empty way of life inherited from your ancestors, not with perishable things like silver or gold, ¹⁹ but with the precious blood of Christ, like that of an unblemished and spotless lamb.

Notes

GOD'S HEART FOR THE VULNERABLE

In the book of Ruth, God used Boaz to care for and meet the needs of Naomi and Ruth, two women whose circumstances left them in a position of vulnerability in their society.

Their story is just one of many examples in Scripture that show God's heart for disempowered or marginalized people. Though God deeply cares about our physical needs, His heart for the vulnerable is not restricted to the physical realm alone. Scripture demonstrates that God draws close to and embraces those who also acknowledge their impoverished spiritual condition. Whether or not someone is physically or socially secure, all people are spiritually poor—needing salvation.

Here you will find just a few examples from Scripture that describe God's heart for both the physically and spiritually vulnerable.

DEUTERONOMY 10:17–18

For the LORD your God is the God of gods and Lord of lords, the great, mighty, and awe-inspiring God, showing no partiality and taking no bribe. He executes justice for the fatherless and the widow, and loves the resident alien, giving him food and clothing.

PSALM 12:5

"Because of the devastation
    of the needy
and the groaning of
    the poor,
I will now rise up," says
    the LORD.
"I will provide safety for the
    one who longs for it."

PROVERBS 14:31

The one who oppresses
    the poor person insults
    his Maker,
but one who is kind to
    the needy honors him.

ISAIAH 41:17

"The poor and the needy
    seek water, but there
    is none;
their tongues are parched
    with thirst.
I will answer them.
I am the LORD, the God
    of Israel. I will not
    abandon them."

MALACHI 3:5

"I will come to you in judgment, and I will be ready to witness against sorcerers and adulterers; against those who swear falsely; against those who oppress the hired worker, the widow, and the fatherless; and against those who deny justice to the resident alien. They do not fear me," says the LORD of Armies.

MATTHEW 5:3

"Blessed are the poor in spirit, for the kingdom of heaven is theirs."

LUKE 4:18–19

"The Spirit of the Lord is
    on me,
because he has
    anointed me
to preach good news to
    the poor.
He has sent me
to proclaim release to
    the captives
and recovery of sight to
    the blind,
to set free the oppressed,
to proclaim the year of the
    Lord's favor."

JOHN 14:18

"I will not leave you as orphans; I am coming to you."

1 CORINTHIANS 1:26–28

Brothers and sisters, consider your calling: Not many were wise from a human perspective, not many powerful, not many of noble birth. Instead, God has chosen what is foolish in the world to shame the wise, and God has chosen what is weak in the world to shame the strong. God has chosen what is insignificant and despised in the world— what is viewed as nothing— to bring to nothing what is viewed as something…

2 CORINTHIANS 8:9

For you know the grace of our Lord Jesus Christ: Though he was rich, for your sake he became poor, so that by his poverty you might become rich.

JAMES 2:5

Listen, my dear brothers and sisters: Didn't God choose the poor in this world to be rich in faith and heirs of the kingdom that he has promised to those who love him?

Ruth and Boaz Marry

RUTH 4:13–17

¹³ Boaz took Ruth and she became his wife. He slept with her, and the Lᴏʀᴅ granted conception to her, and she gave birth to a son. ¹⁴ The women said to Naomi, "Blessed be the Lᴏʀᴅ, who has not left you without a family redeemer today. May his name become well known in Israel.

¹⁵ He will renew your life and sustain you in your old age.

Indeed, your daughter-in-law, who loves you and is better to you than seven sons, has given birth to him." ¹⁶ Naomi took the child, placed him on her lap, and became a mother to him. ¹⁷ The neighbor women said, "A son has been born to Naomi," and they named him Obed. He was the father of Jesse, the father of David.

🔖 GOING DEEPER

ISAIAH 43:1–13

RESTORATION OF ISRAEL

¹ Now this is what the Lᴏʀᴅ says—
the one who created you, Jacob,
and the one who formed you, Israel—
"Do not fear, for I have redeemed you;
I have called you by your name; you are mine.

² When you pass through the waters,
I will be with you,
and the rivers will not overwhelm you.
When you walk through the fire,
you will not be scorched,
and the flame will not burn you.
³ For I am the LORD your God,
the Holy One of Israel, and your Savior.
I have given Egypt as a ransom for you,
Cush and Seba in your place.
⁴ Because you are precious in my sight
and honored, and I love you,
I will give people in exchange for you
and nations instead of your life.
⁵ Do not fear, for I am with you;
I will bring your descendants from the east,
and gather you from the west.
⁶ I will say to the north, 'Give them up!'
and to the south, 'Do not hold them back!'
Bring my sons from far away,
and my daughters from the ends of the earth—
⁷ everyone who bears my name
and is created for my glory.
I have formed them; indeed, I have made them."

⁸ Bring out a people who are blind, yet have eyes,
and are deaf, yet have ears.
⁹ All the nations are gathered together,
and the peoples are assembled.
Who among them can declare this,
and tell us the former things?
Let them present their witnesses
to vindicate themselves,
so that people may hear and say, "It is true."
¹⁰ "You are my witnesses"—
this is the LORD's declaration—
"and my servant whom I have chosen,
so that you may know and believe me
and understand that I am he.
No god was formed before me,
and there will be none after me.
¹¹ I—I am the LORD.
Besides me, there is no Savior.
¹² I alone declared, saved, and proclaimed—
and not some foreign god among you.

So you are my witnesses"—
this is the LORD's declaration—
"and I am God.
¹³ Also, from today on I am he alone,
and none can rescue from my power.
I act, and who can reverse it?"

LUKE 1:67–79

ZECHARIAH'S PROPHECY

⁶⁷ Then his father Zechariah was filled with the Holy Spirit
and prophesied:

⁶⁸ Blessed is the Lord, the God of Israel,
because he has visited
and provided redemption for his people.
⁶⁹ He has raised up a horn of salvation for us
in the house of his servant David,
⁷⁰ just as he spoke by the mouth
of his holy prophets in ancient times;
⁷¹ salvation from our enemies
and from the hand of those who hate us.
⁷² He has dealt mercifully with our ancestors
and remembered his holy covenant—
⁷³ the oath that he swore to our father Abraham,
to grant that we,
⁷⁴ having been rescued
from the hand of our enemies,
would serve him without fear
⁷⁵ in holiness and righteousness
in his presence all our days.
⁷⁶ And you, child, will be called
a prophet of the Most High,
for you will go before the Lord
to prepare his ways,
⁷⁷ to give his people knowledge of salvation
through the forgiveness of their sins.
⁷⁸ Because of our God's merciful compassion,
the dawn from on high will visit us
⁷⁹ to shine on those who live in darkness
and the shadow of death,
to guide our feet into the way of peace.

Notes

RUTH 1:9

May the LORD grant
each of you rest.

Ruth's Legacy

DAVID'S GENEALOGY FROM JUDAH'S SON

18 Now these are the family records of Perez:

Perez fathered Hezron,
19 Hezron fathered Ram,
Ram fathered Amminadab,
20 Amminadab fathered Nahshon,
Nahshon fathered Salmon,
21 Salmon fathered Boaz,
Boaz fathered Obed,
22 Obed fathered Jesse,
and Jesse fathered David.

💙 GOING DEEPER

ISAIAH 11:1–10

REIGN OF THE DAVIDIC KING

1 Then a shoot will grow from the stump of Jesse,
and a branch from his roots will bear fruit.
2 The Spirit of the LORD will rest on him—
a Spirit of wisdom and understanding,
a Spirit of counsel and strength,
a Spirit of knowledge and of the fear of the LORD.
3 His delight will be in the fear of the LORD.
He will not judge
by what he sees with his eyes,
he will not execute justice
by what he hears with his ears,
4 but he will judge the poor righteously
and execute justice for the oppressed of the land.
He will strike the land
with a scepter from his mouth,
and he will kill the wicked
with a command from his lips.
5 Righteousness will be a belt around his hips;
faithfulness will be a belt around his waist.

6 The wolf will dwell with the lamb,
and the leopard will lie down with the goat.
The calf, the young lion, and the fattened calf
will be together,
and a child will lead them.
7 The cow and the bear will graze,
their young ones will lie down together,
and the lion will eat straw like cattle.
8 An infant will play beside the cobra's pit,
and a toddler will put his hand into a snake's den.
9 They will not harm or destroy each other
on my entire holy mountain,
for the land will be as full
of the knowledge of the LORD
as the sea is filled with water.

ISRAEL REGATHERED

10 On that day the root of Jesse
will stand as a banner for the peoples.
The nations will look to him for guidance,
and his resting place will be glorious.

MATTHEW 1:2–16

FROM ABRAHAM TO DAVID

2 Abraham fathered Isaac,
Isaac fathered Jacob,
Jacob fathered Judah and his brothers,
3 Judah fathered Perez and Zerah by Tamar,
Perez fathered Hezron,
Hezron fathered Aram,
4 Aram fathered Amminadab,
Amminadab fathered Nahshon,
Nahshon fathered Salmon,

5 Salmon fathered Boaz by Rahab,
Boaz fathered Obed by Ruth,
Obed fathered Jesse,
6 and Jesse fathered King David.

FROM DAVID TO THE BABYLONIAN EXILE

David fathered Solomon by Uriah's wife,
7 Solomon fathered Rehoboam,
Rehoboam fathered Abijah,

Abijah fathered Asa,
[8] Asa fathered Jehoshaphat,
Jehoshaphat fathered Joram,
Joram fathered Uzziah,
[9] Uzziah fathered Jotham,
Jotham fathered Ahaz,
Ahaz fathered Hezekiah,
[10] Hezekiah fathered Manasseh,
Manasseh fathered Amon,
Amon fathered Josiah,
[11] and Josiah fathered Jeconiah and his brothers
at the time of the exile to Babylon.

FROM THE EXILE TO THE MESSIAH

[12] After the exile to Babylon
Jeconiah fathered Shealtiel,
Shealtiel fathered Zerubbabel,
[13] Zerubbabel fathered Abiud,
Abiud fathered Eliakim,
Eliakim fathered Azor,
[14] Azor fathered Zadok,
Zadok fathered Achim,
Achim fathered Eliud,
[15] Eliud fathered Eleazar,
Eleazar fathered Matthan,
Matthan fathered Jacob,
[16] and Jacob fathered Joseph the husband of Mary,
who gave birth to Jesus who is called the Messiah.

EPHESIANS 2:19–22

[19] So, then, you are no longer foreigners and strangers, but fellow citizens with the saints, and members of God's household, [20] built on the foundation of the apostles and prophets, with Christ Jesus himself as the cornerstone. [21] In him the whole building, being put together, grows into a holy temple in the Lord. [22] In him you are also being built together for God's dwelling in the Spirit.

Final Reflection

BEFORE BEGINNING THIS FINAL REFLECTION, OPEN UP YOUR READER'S EDITION AGAIN AND READ THROUGH THE BOOK OF RUTH ONE MORE TIME.

After reading, use the space on the following pages to journal and respond to the book of Ruth. If you're feeling stuck, use some or all of the questions on the final page as a prompt for your reflection.

Final Reflection

What did this story teach you about God?

What did you notice about how the individuals' lives shifted from the beginning of the story to the end?

Where did you see God's kindness in this book?

How did the people in Ruth's story reflect God's compassion to one another?

How did this story challenge or encourage you?

How do you want to live differently after reading it?

Grace

Take this day to catch
up on your reading, pray,
and rest in the presence
of the Lord.

Day

In him we have
redemption through his
blood, the forgiveness of
our trespasses, according
to the riches of his grace.

———

EPHESIANS 1:7

Weekly Truth

SCRIPTURE IS GOD-BREATHED AND TRUE. WHEN WE MEMORIZE IT, WE CARRY HIS WORD WITH US WHEREVER WE GO.

During our time in this book, we have worked to memorize Ruth 4:14. Continue to repeat it to yourself as a reminder that our God is a God of redemption.

THE WOMEN SAID TO NAOMI, "BLESSED BE
THE LORD, WHO HAS NOT LEFT YOU WITHOUT
A FAMILY REDEEMER TODAY. MAY HIS NAME
BECOME WELL KNOWN IN ISRAEL."

RUTH 4:14

See tips for memorizing Scripture on page 92

Blessed is the Lord, the
God of Israel, because he
has visited and provided
redemption for his people.

———

LUKE 1:68

Tips for Memorizing Scripture

At She Reads Truth, we believe Scripture memorization is an important discipline in your walk with God. Committing God's Truth to memory means He can minister to us—and we can minister to others—through His Word no matter where we are. As you approach the Weekly Truth passage in this book, try these memorization tips to see which techniques work best for you!

STUDY IT

Study the passage in its biblical context and ask yourself a few questions before you begin to memorize it: What does this passage say? What does it mean? How would I say this in my own words? What does it teach me about God? Understanding what the passage means helps you know why it is important to carry it with you wherever you go.

Break the passage into smaller sections, memorizing a phrase at a time.

PRAY IT

Use the passage you are memorizing as a prompt for prayer.

WRITE IT

Dedicate a notebook to Scripture memorization and write the passage over and over again.

Diagram the passage after you write it out. Place a square around the verbs, underline the nouns, and circle any adjectives or adverbs. Say the passage aloud several times, emphasizing the verbs as you repeat it. Then do the same thing again with the nouns, then the adjectives and adverbs.

Write out the first letter of each word in the passage somewhere you can reference it throughout the week as you work on your memorization.

Use a whiteboard to write out the passage. Erase a few words at a time as you continue to repeat it aloud. Keep erasing parts of the passage until you have it all committed to memory.

CREATE

If you can, make up a tune for the passage to sing as you go about your day, or try singing it to the tune of a favorite song.

Sketch the passage, visualizing what each phrase would look like in the form of a picture. Or, try using calligraphy or altering the style of your handwriting as you write it out.

Use hand signals or signs to come up with associations for each word or phrase and repeat the movements as you practice.

SAY IT

Repeat the passage out loud to yourself as you are going through the rhythm of your day—getting ready, pouring your coffee, waiting in traffic, or making dinner.

Listen to the passage read aloud to you.

Record a voice memo on your phone and listen to it throughout the day or play it on an audio Bible.

SHARE IT

Memorize the passage with a friend, family member, or mentor. Spontaneously challenge each other to recite the passage, or pick a time to review your passage and practice saying it from memory together.

Send the passage as an encouraging text to a friend, testing yourself as you type to see how much you have memorized so far.

KEEP AT IT!

Set reminders on your phone to prompt you to practice your passage.

Purchase a She Reads Truth 12 Card Set or keep a stack of notecards with Scripture you are memorizing by your bed. Practice reciting what you've memorized previously before you go to sleep, ending with the passages you are currently learning. If you wake up in the middle of the night, review them again instead of grabbing your phone. Read them out loud before you get out of bed in the morning.

Download the free Weekly Truth lock screens for your phone on the She Reads Truth app and read the passage throughout the day when you check your phone.

CSB BOOK ABBREVIATIONS

OLD TESTAMENT

GN Genesis	**JB** Job	**HAB** Habakkuk	**PHP** Philippians
EX Exodus	**PS** Psalms	**ZPH** Zephaniah	**COL** Colossians
LV Leviticus	**PR** Proverbs	**HG** Haggai	**1TH** 1 Thessalonians
NM Numbers	**EC** Ecclesiastes	**ZCH** Zechariah	**2TH** 2 Thessalonians
DT Deuteronomy	**SG** Song of Solomon	**MAL** Malachi	**1TM** 1 Timothy
JOS Joshua	**IS** Isaiah		**2TM** 2 Timothy
JDG Judges	**JR** Jeremiah		**TI** Titus
RU Ruth	**LM** Lamentations	### NEW TESTAMENT	**PHM** Philemon
1SM 1 Samuel	**EZK** Ezekiel	**MT** Matthew	**HEB** Hebrews
2SM 2 Samuel	**DN** Daniel	**MK** Mark	**JMS** James
1KG 1 Kings	**HS** Hosea	**LK** Luke	**1PT** 1 Peter
2KG 2 Kings	**JL** Joel	**JN** John	**2PT** 2 Peter
1CH 1 Chronicles	**AM** Amos	**AC** Acts	**1JN** 1 John
2CH 2 Chronicles	**OB** Obadiah	**RM** Romans	**2JN** 2 John
EZR Ezra	**JNH** Jonah	**1CO** 1 Corinthians	**3JN** 3 John
NEH Nehemiah	**MC** Micah	**2CO** 2 Corinthians	**JD** Jude
EST Esther	**NAH** Nahum	**GL** Galatians	**RV** Revelation
		EPH Ephesians	

BIBLIOGRAPHY

Barry, John D., David Bomar, Derek R. Brown, Rachel Klippenstein, Douglas Mangum, Carrie Sinclair Wolcott, Lazarus Wentz, Elliot Ritzema, and Wendy Widder, eds. *The Lexham Bible Dictionary*. Bellingham: Lexham Press, 2016.

Brand, Chad, Charles Draper, Archie England, Steve Bond, E. Ray Clendenen, Trent C. Butler, and Bill Latta, eds. *Holman Illustrated Bible Dictionary*. Nashville: Holman Bible Publishers, 2003.

Freedman, David Noel, Gary A. Herion, David F. Graf, John David Pleins, and Astrid B. Beck, eds. *The Anchor Yale Bible Dictionary*. New York: Doubleday, 1992.

LOOKING FOR DEVOTIONALS?

Download the **She Reads Truth app** to find devotionals that complement your daily Scripture reading. If you're stuck on a passage, hop into the community discussion to connect with other Shes who are reading God's Word right along with you. You can also highlight Bible passages and download free lock screens for Weekly Truth memorization—all on the She Reads Truth app.

DOWNLOAD THE
SHE READS TRUTH
APP TODAY!

You just spent 14 days in the Word of God!

MY FAVORITE DAY OF
THIS READING PLAN:

HOW DID I FIND DELIGHT IN GOD'S WORD?

ONE THING I LEARNED
ABOUT GOD:

WHAT WAS GOD DOING IN
MY LIFE DURING THIS STUDY?

WHAT DID I LEARN THAT I WANT TO SHARE
WITH SOMEONE ELSE?

A SPECIFIC SCRIPTURE THAT
ENCOURAGED ME:

A SPECIFIC SCRIPTURE THAT
CHALLENGED AND CONVICTED ME: